ASIAN SURVIVORS OF

DOMESTIC VIOLENCE

Edward Charles Adams

Social Work Monographs, Norwich

First published 1998

Monograph No. 166

ISBN 1 85784 065 8

ACKNOWLEDGEMENTS

I should like to thank the Director of WAITS, Joan Blaney, and their Domestic Violence Worker, Kulbinder Kaur, for their advice, assistance and support in undertaking this study and their help with the questionnaire and with conducting the survey. I should also like to thank Evelyn Stanley for her help in the survey. Peter Stokes of Community Resource in Birmingham was also both usefully critical and unfailingly supportive. Finally, I wish to say how encouraged I was by the sympathetic but not uncritical help and advice from Harriet Ward.

This Monograph was originally submitted in part fulfilment of the requirements for the degree of Master of Arts in Social Work at the University of Leicester.

Ed Adams is now working as a Probation Officer for Leicestershire Probation Service

CONTENTS

INTRODUCTION

A personal introduction to the Director of WAITS (Women Acting in Today's Society), at a time when this dynamic voluntary organisation was preparing for a significant symposium on domestic violence in several ethnic communities in Birmingham led to this study. It appeared that, perhaps for the first time in the United Kingdom, an open debate had begun which was giving public voice to the experience and views of women from ethnic communities who had undergone domestic violence.

This symposium and its report reflected a growing documentation on the subject in recent years, urging statutory agencies to empower women experiencing violence to make their voices heard. This was one of the principal findings of another recent MA thesis which urged 'the incorporation into social work practice of a feminist approach to woman battering...through focusing on the process of empowering the battered woman to perceive herself as the 'expert' on her situation' (McCann, 1995: ii).

A report from Leicester was also published in that year (Belgrave Baheno. 1995), whilst The Southall Black Sisters have recently produced a collection of their reports and briefings on these issues over a number of years in the form of a Domestic Violence Information Pack (no date). It seemed too significant a series of coincidences to miss such an opportunity to review the current situation, assess the realities of present social work theory and practice and consider possible future directions for both.

Definitions

In the interest of clarity the reader should bear in mind that the following definitions apply throughout this Monograph:

Asian

People of south Asian descent in the United Kingdom, in particular of Bangladeshi, Indian or Pakistani descent.

Conscientisation

A psycho-social learning process of praxis (i.e. reflection and action) by which people come to an awareness of their own consciousness and reality through the realisation and solution of their problems in their own terms as joint-players rather than traditional teachers-learners.

Culture

The historical legacy, appearance, use of language, family structure, beliefs, attitudes, arts and social practices which are shared by a body of people.

Domestic Violence

The repeated, habitual or random use of aggression, whether physical, verbal, social, sexual, emotional, psychological or economic, by an individual on a partner or ex-partner in an existing or previous domestic relationship to force submission to that person s demands, thus depriving the partner of personal liberty and basic human rights.

Ethnic Minority

People in the United Kingdom of African. Asian. Arabic, or African Caribbean descent who form minority groups of distinct cultural identities.

Patriarchy

A system of society wherein men have all or most of the power.

Survivor

The person who has experienced domestic violence at the hands of a perpetrator. It has to be noted however that not all such persons do survive.

The Aims and Objectives of the Research

Domestic violence is now a relatively well documented phenomenon within the social work sphere. It is only recently, however, that domestic violence within the ethnic minority communities in the United Kingdom has begun to be open for debate. The reluctance to acknowledge its existence within the ethnic minorities has probably been even more pronounced than within the White European community.

From what is written about Asian cultures in the United Kingdom, it seems logical to expect that the pattern and experience of domestic violence would, in certain respects, differ from that in white cultures. The results from the first open conference on the subject, for example, indicated that many women in these communities who had suffered abuse had faced additional pressures that stem from and are specific to their culture (WAITS 1995). Around half of the women surveyed cited cultural reasons for staying with their partner. These included concerns about their families and communities and the associated feelings of bringing disgrace upon one's family if one was disloyal enough to seek outside help. Additional discrimination was also encountered when confronted with culturally ignorant, insensitive, and sometimes racist services.

Research Statement and Methodology

A review of the literature on domestic violence was made and related to some theories of social work. Special attention was given to more recent studies on domestic violence in the Asian and African Caribbean black communities in the United Kingdom in order to present as up to date a picture of the current scene as possible. Negotiations were held with the Director and the Domestic Violence Worker based in the Birmingham voluntary agency WAITS (Women Acting in Today's Society) and a questionnaire devised. The questionnaire was designed to test various hypotheses, which were based

3

on the above review and discussions with people who worked in the field. These hypotheses were:

I.   There is more reluctance on the part of Asian women to admit they are victims of domestic violence.

2.   Asian women experience greater family and social pressures to maintain silence in the face of domestic violence.

3.   Asian women suffer longer than white women before seeking help outside the family.

4.   There is an absence of culture-specific aid agencies for Asian women and inadequate practical help.

5.   Culture-specific voluntary agencies, with training in the field, are the best response to the issue.

To this end two groups of ten survivors were chosen - one Asian and one White European. Due to the size of the sample, the findings could not be justifiably generalised to Asian women or White European women as a whole. However, they provide anecdotal evidence and throw light on general areas of difference, and similarity between the groups as well as picking up common themes through the responses given by both groups. In this way, once the responses had been analysed, an indication might be gained on the validity of the proposed hypotheses. Some tentative conclusions could be drawn and discussed alongside the experience of the research study as a whole.

Both sets of interviews were conducted by women from the same cultures as the survivors. The Asian interviewer was the Domestic Violence Worker for WAITS. She interviewed most Asian women in and from an Asian refuge where she once worked, and others who were known to her by her involvement in the Asian Women's Network. This had initially been set up by WAITS as an

employment and educational project to increase opportunities for Asian women. However, the increased confidence women gained through this project led to personal issues arising and being discussed - including domestic violence.

The White European interviews were conducted by a woman who works in the Domestic Violence Department of a solicitor's office. Interviews were conducted there, and also on community-based projects. It is important to note that some of the White European women. when commenting on such things as the treatment they received would have been referring to the interviewer.

Thus, due to where and by whom the interviews were undertaken, differences emerge between the two sample groups which are not attributable to race, colour or culture. An obvious example of this is that more of the Asian survivors had sought and received help from refuges than White European survivors. In the same way, more of the latter group had had involvement with solicitors. It may be that this is a pattern repeated, albeit to a lesser extent, among their respective groups as a whole, but the size of the samples means that no light could be thrown on that particular question. Probably the most important difference to note though, is that because of the interview settings many of the White European women had reached the stage of taking legal steps against their partners. Many of the Asian women, in contrast, had only recently escaped from their partner and the violence. One Asian woman was still in a violent relationship. On some sections of the questionnaire therefore, the White European women's responses may be more positive due to them having had more time to regain control over their lives and come to terms with what had happened.

It is inevitable that, however much time and work is spent in the design of a questionnaire, upon completion of the interviews and when the data is being analysed one will find inadequacies and flaws,

and think of questions one would have liked to have asked or ask differently in order to gain a clearer picture. This survey has been no different.

One example of this is that the author had assumed the violence and abuse would come solely from the survivor's male partner. The question which was not asked was "Who abused you". While in all cases this would have included the male partner, most probably as the main perpetrator, it is the case that some women, and in particular Asian women, also suffer violence and abuse from other family members. These could include in-laws, possibly blaming them for the state of their marriage and the resulting abuse itself. However, the responses gained from other questions give us an insight into the family dynamics at work and how much of a role they played.

Chapter five contains the main points which arose out of an analysis of the questionnaire responses.

The Prevalence of Domestic Violence in the United Kingdom - An Outline
According to the 1992 British Crime Survey 11% of women who had lived with a partner had at some time experienced physical violence from a partner (Mirrlees-Black, 1995). Nearly half (46%) of all violent incidents against women in 1991 were 'domestic' on a broad definition covering physical violence from partners, ex-partners, relatives and current household members. On these criteria, at least 190,000 women experienced one or more incidents of domestic violence in that year. Half of these experienced more than one attack, a third experienced three or more. In total, the survey estimated that 460,000 of the 530,000 incidents of domestic violence (87%) were against women. Of the latter, 54% of the incidents involved a current partner and 36% an ex-partner.

Younger women appeared to be at greater risk than those over 30. Though treatment of this issue as a phenomenon among manual workers or the unemployed has been criticised, notably by Smith, 'households in which domestic violence was reported to have occurred did tend to be the more socio-economically deprived' (1989: 4).

The BCS figure is generally regarded as underestimating the situation, as most surveys are likely to do given the nature of the phenomenon. Morley and Mullender, for example, in a 1994 Home Office report, quote a figure of 30% of women experiencing physical violence from partners. Higher percentages such as this appear due to a wider definition of the term domestic violence. The advantage of the BCS survey is its large nationally representative sample and relatively high response rate which offers reliable detail. Further support for such an estimate comes from a recent Merseyside Probation Service survey with a sample of 298 cases which revealed a similar figure (10%) (Stelman 1993).

A much smaller study undertaken on a London Housing Estate adds an interesting footnote to the BCS findings -the authors conclude that:

> (the study) suggests that domestic violence is not something which only affects the marginalised, but 'ordinary' people, and it may even be seen as part of ordinary life. This climate of acceptance ensures that few will seek the assistance of statutory agencies and that those that do will first have to overcome their conviction that they brought the violence on themselves. (Bush and Hood-Williams, 1995: 17)

Such a specific view and such an overall picture provide a context for examining the nature and prevalence of domestic violence within the United Kingdom's ethnic minority communities.

THE CURRENT EXPERIENCE OF DOMESTIC VIOLENCE IN THE UNITED KINGDOM'S ETHNIC MINORITY COMMUNITIES PLACED IN A CULTURAL PERSPECTIVE

As has already been indicated, initial interest in this issue arose from what was probably the first open event focusing on domestic violence in ethnic minority communities promoted by the West Midlands community organising agency WAITS. In their report of their consultation day, reviewing the findings of their study and giving a voice to the views of several survivors of domestic violence, WAITS suggest that there is a growing number of reported incidents of this nature from 10,350 in 1992 to 12,679 in 1994. Approximately 15% of these incidents involved members of ethnic minority communities (in line with a 14.6% ethnic minority population in the area according to the latest census figures). These data need to be read in conjunction with other studies which indicate that only a very small percentage of such incidents get reported to the police. Dobash and Dobash (1979) suggest as few as 2%, although the Manushi Report suggests as many as 23%.

Both the WAITS and the Manushi Reports provide useful current evidence. The picture to emerge from the WAITS study of 70 survivors of domestic violence included specific references to them experiencing:

- difficulty in expressing their feelings

- insensitivity and a lack of awareness of cultural needs and differences

- fears of social repercussions from relatives and friends

- a lack of knowledge of services and resources available to them

- a dearth of refuges and a lack of adequate financing and staffing therein

- racism and feelings of imprisonment in refuges.

A specifically Asian perspective was illustrated by one case study which read: 'when I came to England I found it very hard to cope and missed my friends and family... Since I could not speak English I could not talk to anyone. The neighbours and other people were always on my husband's side'. Problems of language and ignorance or lack of resources and services were a major reason for remaining in violent relationships - reasons confirmed in this study. 'I didn't know of any help available'. 'I was imprisoned in my own home'. 'Learn to speak English and make friends to find information of what is available to women'. In the WAITS survey half of the respondents experienced domestic violence for up to five years before they sought help; 38% remained in such relationships for between five and ten years, whilst several had experienced violence for over 20 years. Fewer survivors in this study appear to have remained as long. This would seem worth further investigation and might reflect a growing unwillingness to tolerate abuse. The major factor which eventually induced the women in the WAITS survey to leave was a fear for the safety of their children or themselves. Even with all these limiting factors, only 20% of survivors indicated that their departures were planned. Both of these findings tally with the views expressed by the survivors in this study.

There was almost no prior knowledge of the existence of refuges (only 6% of respondents sought initial help from them), with most recourse for help being sought from police domestic violence units (25%), friends (20%) and local authority neighbourhood offices (a feature of Birmingham City Council's local government – 17%): 38% reported no contact with any support service. Of those who did seek assistance, 55% described this as poor but the remainder experienced a 'satisfactory or very good response'. The responses in this survey would suggest that the balance may have shifted a little: 60% indicated very or fairly positive assistance.

The Manushi Report draws attention to the relative lack of information on Asian women and domestic violence and was based on a study of the experiences of 68 women and 57 agency comments. This study, conducted in Leicester, found that only 25% of those experiencing violence received any help from support services despite a level of violence which affected 90% of them on a daily or weekly basis. The findings in this survey were more positive.

Other relevant evidence from the Manushi Report was that 34 respondents reported that they knew another 240 women who had experienced domestic violence; the average length of the respondents' experience of violence was 11.3 years, which probably bears relation to the WAITS study although it is significantly higher than that found in this survey; many of the women had attempted to leave their situations up to seven times before finally doing so: - 8% of them sought help as soon as they knew it was available; more than twice as many of them experienced violence when in their thirties as when in their twenties (contrary to the BCS finding); and more than half needed an interpreter to understand English. Only 14% of the Manushi respondents had sought initial support from an agency whilst 16% had first approached family or friends. From amongst those who eventually did seek agency assistance, 14% went first to the police, which was a much lower percentage than in the WAITS study (25%). This may reflect the greater development and acceptance of the West Midlands Police's Domestic Violence Units. Perhaps as a consequence there was a greater reliance on refuges as a first source of help, while the reliance on solicitors and Asian Women's organisations was on a par with that found by WAITS. The findings of this study, subject to the caveats already made, somewhat paradoxically would seem to support both the Manushi and the WAITS reports: a heavy involvement with refuges but also support from the police on a par with that found by WAITS.

Further evidence of the experience of domestic violence by Asian women is provided by the report based on fourteen years work by Southall Black Sisters (no date). The Sisters claim to handle over one thousand enquiries every year from women and young girls, the majority of whom are from the Indian sub-continent. 'The vast majority' are experiencing domestic violence and 'many' had come forward after years of having tried to stay in their relationships in spite of undergoing regular abuse (ibid: 6). The range of these years was from three to forty, with an average of ten, which in turn corresponds with the findings of the previous studies to which reference has been made.

III

AN ASIAN DIMENSION TO DOMESTIC VIOLENCE – TRADITIONS AND MODERN REACTIONS

Mama refers to the long history in Asia of patriarchal practices, such as suttee and dowry deaths, that have been very damaging to women (1989: 5-6). For centuries there has been widespread violence and abuse of wives by husbands, policemen, landowners and in-laws arising out of an 'hierarchical gender relationship, where men are dominant and women are subordinate'. 'Possessional rights' are assumed which 'include the promise of protection in return for submission and exclusive use '. The process of socialisation in many Asian societies 'embeds women strongly within the familial structure and hierarchic gender relations such that they have little or no independent status and transgressions outside the family and male authority expose them to swift retributions and confirm their vulnerability'. 'Violence against women then is fundamentally about enforcing power relations between men and women. There is, however, a strong class-caste component'. Mass rapes of women have also been a means whereby landlords and government officials repress families of labourers and peasants. Thus violence against women in Asian communities has a tradition of being embedded in forms of state and economic oppression and exploitation.

There is modern evidence, according to Mama, that women continue to be burned to death because their families cannot meet dowry demands - and that no police action ensued. There is also a legacy of 'servitude and sexploitation' which 'is a direct product of both colonial and military history and economic relations'. It would seem that there is at present an extensive debate within Asian communities, particularly within the United Kingdom, about the origins of these practices and the reason for their persistence. This debate extends to the legitimacy of their persistence.

In her illuminating study of the place of women in Moroccan society, for example, Mernissi attributes the origins to, and blames their persistence on, Islam (1975). However, Muslim apologists for the cause of women, argue that family and social practices inimical to women derive from the secular customs prevailing at the time during which societies came to accept Islam (see Amin, 1928).

Mernissi argues that whilst this belief in equality was indeed asserted it was also regarded as a danger which necessitated a divinely inspired, and hence unchangeable, family structure shackling this potential power for independence. For Mernissi, 'Muslim ideology, which views men and women as enemies, tries to separate the two, and empowers men with institutionalised means to oppress women' (ibid xvi-xvii). Love between men and women can be regarded as a threat to the primacy of the man s allegiance to Allah. Thus there has arisen 'a set of laws and customs which ensure that women's status remains one of subjugation. Prime amongst these are the family laws based on male authority' (ibid: viii).

The Koran recommends a Muslim who is upset by his wife to scold her and, if necessary, stop having sexual relations with her. If these measures fail then he has a 'right' to beat her - but only as a last resort and in 'decent' degree. The Koran also contains instructions about sexual relations which certainly lead a detached observer to an understanding of Mernissi's emphasis on the threat to a man's relationship with Allah which women must pose. The prevalence in the past of polygamy, practised by Mohammed himself, also seems rooted in this need to reduce the emotional ties between man and wife. In any event, it would seem that polyandry has never featured as a Muslim practice.

Another Muslim tenet which profoundly affects wife/husband relationships is the importance placed on the relationship between a mother and her son. Thus, says Mernissi. 'in Muslim societies, not only is

the marital bond actually weakened and love for the wife discouraged., but his mother is the only woman a man is allowed to love at all, and this love is encouraged to take the form of life-long gratitude' (ibid: 69). Traditionally mothers have a decisive role in the choice of brides for their sons and are guides for their daughters-in-law. This has often led to significant domination over the newly-weds' household to the extent that Mernissi concludes that 'the triangle of mother, son and wife is the trump card in the Muslim pack of legal, ideological and physical barriers which subordinate the wife to the husband and condemn the heterosexual relation to mistrust, violence and deceit' (ibid: 79).

For Mernissi the Muslim family is characterised by inequality, lack of reciprocity, segregation, separation and division, subordination and authority, and mistrust. However, past cultures are giving way under modern social and economic demands. It is thus impossible to segregate the sexes as much as was previously felt to be 'proper' and this phenomenon has encouraged women to reject a subordinate, all-accepting role. Education and more economic independence enhances such feelings. All these factors have increased the pressures on Muslim men not socialised traditionally to woo women through love and badly equipped to meet potential partners as self-determining equals.

The Muslim marriage:

> is based on the premise that social order can only be maintained if the women's dangerous potential for chaos is restrained by a dominating non-loving husband who has besides his wife, other females (concubines, co-wives and prostitutes) available for his sexual pleasure under equally degrading conditions A new sexual order based on the absence of all dehumanising limitations of the woman's potential means the destruction of the traditional Muslim family. In this respect, fears embedded in the culture through centuries of women's oppression and associated with changes in the family and the woman's condition are justified. (Mernissi. ibid: 101)

Although this is one theory of Islam in practice. it is a view not shared by all adherents. Some modern Muslim women would question Mernissi's thesis and follow Amin s line that many of the customs of Asian family life derive from cultural traditions and practice (BBC Radio I, 1995). Thus to oppose customs, institutions and practices which encourage women s segregation, ignorance and exclusion does not violate Islam which, it is asserted, legalised equality between the sexes and asserted women's freedom at a time when this was rarely acknowledged elsewhere. What appears to have happened is that many Muslims in the United Kingdom have brought village traditions from rural, farming communities which, in an insular community life in Britain, have assumed a formal and quasi-religious authority and an almost tribal exclusiveness. Many such families remain relatively unsophisticated as they pass on by word of mouth a culture so rooted in the past that it no longer relates to that now found in many of these same villages back in Asia. The Koran is learnt in a ritual, parrot-like fashion and nationality and ethnicity are put before Islam. The correct teachings of the Koran remain unknown through parental ignorance and lack of education. Thus the Islamic concept of 'haraam', they argue, expressly forbids arranged marriage without the consent of the pair to be married. Marriages must be entered freely and willingly, with couples able to write their own contracts. Such contracts can include an automatic right to divorce for either partner should one of them wish it. Within a family it would indeed be a matter of izzat (honour), so often cited as oppressive for women, to ensure that female members of the family should know and act upon this right.

For these apologists, therefore, tribal custom, nationality, and ethnicity are seen as having usurped true Islam at whose heart is diversity, equality, mercy and compassion. For them it is not a certain, rigid path but a faith which encourages personal choice, thinking and reflection including the independence of women. Thus many Muslims are unaware of the freedom of thought that their faith allows. All believers are equal and enjoy a personal relationship with Allah that does not require any intermediary such as a priest. Women can perform all Islamic religious rites. The Koran and certainly the Suni laws which cover 85% of Muslims would support women s opposition to the impositions of men such as forced marriages and domestic violence.

It is important to be aware of this debate which seems likely to become more widespread and vehement in the future. Whatever attitude one may take, however, it remains clear that modern Asian women have inherited, by history, religion, culture, education, economics and politics a heavy burden. For many in the United Kingdom there are problems of money, social isolation and racism but on top of these go factors of family and cultural life which influence their experience of domestic violence.

Many of the United Kingdom's Asian women have, in recent years, been experiencing the pressures on and the disintegration of the traditional patterns of family life. Sexual segregation and subjugation to the mother-in-law have diminished. Where the latter have remained, economic, social and media influences have encouraged many women to react against them. Wife-husband interaction has increased and sexually antagonistic traditions, tensions and fears, previously borne in secret or seen as incapable of resolution, have exploded. Economic pressures on male employment can encourage questioning of the man as the provider, whilst education and more liberal attitudes to the role of women in the white communities encourage ideas of rights for women as women. The pressures for tension increase again and are further exacerbated by western ideals of marriages based on romantic love and mutual respect.

So far in this review the impact of religion has been confined to that of Islam. However, though Sikhism is meant to be a religion of reform and many Sikh women now go to work:

they rarely make, or are consulted about, decisions made about money. After listening to my Sikh sisters accounts of their lives and relationships and the sensitive izzat of their men I had the feeling that for Sikhs izzat is not pride or honour - it is male ego pure and simple. (Wilson. 1978: 41)

In Hinduism there is also an emphasis on women's domestic role. Wilson quotes from Manu the lawgiver twelve centuries ago that 'the chief function of a woman is to give birth, nurse those who are born and attend daily duties' (1978: 3). Hindus and Sikhs have taken over the concept of izzat from the Muslims as the Muslims and Sikhs have adopted the dowry system from the Hindus.

The Southall Black Sisters claim that 'it is quite common for (Asian) women to adopt and borrow traditions freely from the different cultures that they are exposed to' (no date: 16). What appears to be accepted, moreover, is that whatever the culture there is a stereotyped attitude in statutory agencies, such as Social Service Department, Health Authorities and the Police, that regards the family as firmly within the sphere of whatever dominant interpretation of culture and religion prevails. What follows is a reluctance to examine class, caste or gender issues within ethnic minority communities, and in particular the power relations between men and women. 'State agencies', say the Southall Black Sisters, 'in an effort to appear multicultural and even anti-racist, are often reluctant to intervene where Asian women are concerned. Guided by the belief that the Asian community have their own internal mechanisms to resolve marital problems, they often deny Asian women the same advice and help offered to other women (ibid).

In spite of some of the modernising trends within the Asian community in the United Kingdom, to which reference was made earlier, many families retain a tendency to social isolation. This has meant that Asian women have continued to experience the male-dominated cultural practices which tradition

17

has brought. Opinions among Asian women may differ about Mernissi's view of the influence of Islam on these practices. Most Asian communities in the United Kingdom today, however, would still have an ideal for women to be dutiful, obedient and self-sacrificial. A likely fate for women who seek to be independent is to be labelled as unworthy, or worse, and corrupted by western values.

Sita, the wife of the Hindu god Ram, symbolises this ideal which is also epitomised by the historical Muslim practice of suttee, wherein widows follow their husbands to death by throwing themselves on the latter's funeral pyres, to which earlier reference was made. Notions of izzat, of which a brief mention has also been given, and sharam (shame) also tend to be followed in ways which oppress women rather than in the positive or more neutral fashion which it was earlier suggested should be the case.

Izzat is graphically defined by Wilson thus – 'the sensitive and many-faceted male family identity which can change as the situation demands it - from family pride to honour to self-respect, and sometimes to pure male ego" (1978: 31). Izzat is under such constant threat and stress from an essentially white, capitalist, racist society with modest or absent regard for Asian cultures and family values that Asian women often become, as Wilson puts it, 'the scapegoats of damaged izzat" (1978: 32). Once izzat is stained family feuds can become generational, crossing from Asia to the United Kingdom.

The most fundamental objection to arranged marriages is that they are a part of the gigantic, oppressive framework of the joint family which has subjugated women for centuries - they are 'no happy commune made up of equal partners. They are an hierarchy economically and in terms of power, one to which the oppression of women is basic. Right at the bottom of the hierarchy is the new bride' (Wilson. 1978: 117). Thus as she again summarises -women's 'roles are in a state of flux, with the past,

the peasant past, the tribal past, the colonial past each with its own particular prescription for the women's role constantly intruding into the present' (1978: 15). The place of women in Islamic, Hindu and Sikh cultures is in this way constantly in change from within and without: as in the dominant white culture except more so.

Cultures exist and have their purposes - solidarity, mutual support, boundaries and norms, maintenance of historical ties, meanings and achievements and so on. But they exact their price, usually in terms of conservatism and restriction. In times of rapid change they can be havens or dungeons. Immigrant communities have tried to re-establish their cultures in alien territory among people many of whom have experienced, and still experience, the cataclysmic change of a second industrial and technological revolution. There has been no settled and welcoming climate in which to find their place and they too have undergone, and continue to undergo, all the effects of formidable industrial recession and change. Since many immigrants arrived to take up residence in inner-city areas facing housing shortages and dilapidation, and work in declining industries or threatened public services such as the health service, these difficulties were multiplied several fold. The ages and occupational skills of the Asian population have meant that it has been disproportionately affected by both these economic changes and by government policies with regard to the young, the working class and inner-cities.

Even when there is a more accepting attitude to Asian survivors of domestic violence sometimes it is conditional and fails to acknowledge a woman's right to determine her own destiny without any limitations imposed by religion, culture or nationality. In the experience of the Southall Black Sisters, there have been those who see the provision of help to survivors as a means of keeping Muslim women isolated from the effects of other religions, secular western influences and alien values (1990: 27). Others see refuges as places of re-education or adjustment to required cultural norms, usually of a

19

conservative and male-dominated order. Furthermore, segregated refuges can be viewed merely as places of asylum to allow tempers and feelings to calm down and women eventually to be restored to their families. This is, indeed, within the WAITS experience. Sometimes this can be a worthwhile, honourable and just goal. It has, however, to be a goal that is acceptable to the survivors and not a condition of residence. Refuges need to be regarded not merely as places of asylum, important as that is, but as opportunities to rebuild or establish enough self-confidence, independence and worth for women not only to cope in life but to play meaningful and influential roles in fashioning life for themselves and others after their own values.

This issue raises a crucial question. As Sahgal writes:

> Black women were to be celebrated when they came out in their thousands to oppose the presence of fascists in their streets, but not when they tried to create a new movement and consciousness and challenged the notion of a unified community. (1990: 1 7)

This was because the Southall Black Sisters broke the silence of the ethnic minority communities on the domestic violence perpetrated by black men on black women. It was felt that to acknowledge such a phenomenon would, in the words of Parmar, 'reinforce ideas of Asian men being more sexist than white men and Asian families being particularly barbaric and tyrannical' (1982). Saghal states: 'our agendas were structured by the threat of the bogey of the liberal racist. To attempt to raise awkward issues publicly was to transgress' (op. cit: 20).

Thus domestic violence in Asian communities can be obscured by ideas of national, cultural, religious and community loyalties on top of family loyalties. There is yet another drawback, however, which exacerbates this problem. This is the white feminist argument, perhaps now in the process of wider modification in the light of black women's experiences, that the family is per se an oppressive institution for women. The argument is based on the view that families have by their nature to be

The mean dimension

male-dominated and focussed. For some black women the struggles of their female ancestors against slavery had been to retain their right to live as families. Among Asian women the idea that arranged marriages are a mere addendum to the issue of marriage as an oppressive institution has often been too hard a concept to accept. For many Asian women, as for women from other ethnic minorities, white feminist jargon from a lesbian perspective has proved extremely alienating and intimidating. This is a point made by WAITS.

One further factor of significant moment for Asian survivors of domestic violence is the influence of British immigration law. Such is the nature of this law and the way it is interpreted and operated that the risk of deportation leads many women with no alternative but to put up with violence. Rules based on the current legislation, for example, require a woman applying for residence in the United Kingdom on the basis of marriage to remain within that marriage for at least a year before she is given the right to stay indefinitely - the 'one year rule'.

This situation provides the settled family with the:

> opportunity to use their position of power to exploit the vulnerability and insecurity of the dependent spouse... Marriage is often treated by the settled spouse as 'trial' marriage... if they do not approve of their partner, they can utilise the rule as a convenient route to dispense with the 'unwanted' spouse. (Southall Black Sisters, no date: 26)

To add to the pressures on women not to complain or leave there is the prospect that deportation is unlikely to lead to a welcome home from a caring and concerned family but rather a reception of hostility, failure, discrimination as an outcast, destitution, sexual exploitation and other forms of violence. Such is the lack of knowledge of immigration rules on the part of many new brides that they are reduced to total dependence on their spouses for an understanding of the possibilities of employment. They may have little or no English of their own to discover their rights or opportunities.

This is in addition to feelings of failed hopes and expectations shame and humiliation. Should women in such situations be aware of their legal situation they then have to contend with the condition of residence which stipulates that they should be no claim on the public purse during their first year in this country. The WAITS experience reinforces the relevance and influence of these factors. The survey outlined in chapter five provides evidence that these factors genuinely exist - "I am told that I am not entitled to any income support because I have not been in this country long enough. I am told to return to my husband or go back to Pakistan". "I am planning to leave the country soon and go back home to escape from violence".

IV

THE RELEVANCE OF SOCIAL WORK THEORIES IN A CROSS-CULTURAL PERSPECTIVE AND SOME OF THEIR IMPLICATIONS FOR SOCIAL WORK PRACTICE

In reviewing social work theories in the context of domestic violence the approach of conscientious. (see p.5) stands out. It is important, however, to look at what other theories may have to offer to social workers confronting this issue, and to attest to the belief that social workers should always be ready to draw on whatever insights any theory can contribute to their understanding and skills, either in general or on a given issue.

The <u>psycho-analytic or psycho-therapeutic</u> theories of social work offer the positive ideal of improving clients self-knowledge. They do this through the exploration of experiences and emotions, a consequent interpretation by the social worker/ therapist and an assessment of the resultant changes which this process brings. According to the specific school of thought there is some. if not a strong, emphasis on the interpretation of childhood memories and emotions.

Difficulties with this approach to social work practice in situations of domestic violence arise from the links it maintains with the medical model of diagnosis and treatment from a given base of knowledge and expertise held by the social worker. The prevailing attitudes to women in society at the time of Freud has coloured much analytic theory to this day. The result was a whole body of theory around the concept of penis envy and female masochism. Yet further complications arising for workers thinking of using analytical insights come from the stereotyping of women and their role in society; even with the modifications of later analysts there seems to be little real recognition of women as men's equals. Indeed the whole culture of analysis occasions the view that it is a conformist ideology which places its

practitioners in a strait jacket, as god-like figures without whom significant personal or inter-personal problems are impossible to resolve. In this process clients can become dependent on therapy in addition to feeling disempowered and unable to resolve difficulties for themselves.

The notion of therapy in itself carries the implication that clients need to conform to some cultural ideal in order to avoid the problems that confront them. Therapy can thus be regarded as an agent of the prevailing, conservative forces in society seeking to preserve the status quo. Clients are offered few perspectives on sex-role conditioning, racism or socio-economic-environmental issues such as poverty, and it may be argued, clients are led to conform to the ideas which the therapists hold about the nature of society and one's place in it. In addition, the prevailing insights of analysis seem to follow a medical model with an emphasis on a pathology of survivors of domestic violence which incorporates ideas of provocation as well as masochism Male violence, it is said, springs from men's reactions to women's attempts at controlling or castrating behaviour.

What might be of use to workers from psycho-analytic and psycho-therapeutic approaches, however, subject to all the caveats above and those that follow, will be the more general insights of the idea of defence mechanisms, the influence of past experiences on present behaviour and the effects of unresolved anxieties that have all influenced social casework. .Psycho-analysis has also given rise to the development of an understanding of human psychology, personality and behaviour with ideas of defences such as repression, projection, denial and displacement, with importance being given to experiences of loss, separation, pain and anxiety, with ideas of the growth of the ego and concepts such as ambivalence, resistance and transference. The importance analysis gives to the free association of ideas has also influenced the non-judgmental approach and the idea of letting clients tell their own stories which is vital for social work with survivors. Such of these insights and knowledge which can

24

assist social workers to gain a better understanding of survivors and a fulfilment of their role with them should be used. This thesis of an eclecticism firmly ensconced in an overall philosophy which recognises the political and cultural factors which shape people's lives and a role for the social worker as an educator for liberation on the Freire model will be further developed as this study progresses.

The insights of Carl Rogers and the interactionist approach to social work, however, has more to offer workers seeking to understand the situation of clients in domestic violence situations and assist in the resolution of both immediate and long-term problems. This approach emphasises mutual understanding and support. It seeks to avoid the directive tendencies inherent in the more analytically orientated therapies. Its fundamental tenet is that human beings have an inner drive to self-realisation. Given right relationships this happens. When there is distress the social worker's relationship is the means whereby it is relieved. For workers these theories emphasise the need to develop 'a trusting, nurturing and long-term relationship' with clients (Wallis, 1973: 80). Following the work of Hollis (1964) the basis of such relationships is support, sustainment, the exploration and ventilation of feelings, and reflection. It is a critical skill for social workers to be able to develop and sustain these relationships. The importance of the use of reflection is something to which further attention and emphasis will be added when the contribution of Paolo Freire to this study is assessed (1972 [1] and [2]; Taylor, 1993). Such an approach fits in well with what seems to lie at the heart of the work of peer group agencies such as WAITS.

The interactionist approach nonetheless is in danger of retaining connotations of manipulation and control, with workers acting as 'special people with authority, knowledge and prestige to command and control' (Rowe, 1993: 13). Mutual understanding and support often seem to degenerate in the

counselling approach of the interactionists through a failure to incorporate them within a social, cultural and politico-economic dynamic.

<u>Behavioural theory, problem-solving approaches, task-centred methods and the techniques of crisis intervention</u> would all seem to have something to offer the social worker in situations of domestic violence provided notions of blame or failure on the part of the person being abused are avoided. Ideas of respondent or operant conditioning if not used tactfully could prove unacceptable to such clients or to those who may surround them. The key contribution of this approach would be to encourage a change in the ineffective or self-defeating responses to the unwanted stimuli of violence both through conditioning and through the introduction., through peer group organisations such as WAITS, of social learning and modelling. This would need to be done whilst avoiding the imposition of ideas of failure to measure up to some theoretical model of a norm of adequacy in social functioning. Individual pathology and failures in socialisation, as well as the breakdown of relationships and family systems, have their part to play in the phenomenon of domestic violence, however much one would feel it right and necessary to emphasise the importance of breakdowns and failures in the proper functioning of modern western social structures.

Where one would wish to question functionalist theories, however, is in any tendency to regard the role of the social worker as that of accommodating clients to the requirements or needs of the state. It has to be recognised and accepted that social workers are bound by the laws governing agency practice and the rules and objectives that have been set in their conditions of service. As Howe describes, social work is a 'largely state-sponsored, agency based, organisationally-tethered activity... (a) formidable context' (1991: 204). We all have to reach a modus vivendi in our relationship with the society around us, but this process should be regarded as dynamic and involving issues of conflict, power and self

realisation as much as co-operation and mutual understanding. Self-interest and the realisation of one's talents is not an ignoble vision. Nor will all those with power wish to share it from motives of altruism, human sympathy or understanding.

For what Howe terms the radical-humanist approach to social work the emphasis shifts to a greater awareness of how the culture of the society in which we grow up shapes our being - our senses, our views and our vision. The social worker's role, therefore, is to work alongside clients and help them understand the forces which have permeated their lives and shaped them into their current fashion - in behaviour, relationships, attitudes... Some would regard this approach as optimistic but it would seem more apt to describe it as based in realism, and one would not see the need to draw any rigid dichotomy between this view and those who lay stress on individual failings or frailties. Nor need there be any dichotomy in the idea of a social worker with a breadth of knowledge, skills and experience of social work (i.e. a professional) working alongside clients to help find solutions to crises in their lives.

An added and specific perspective to this approach, however, is provided by a feminist theory for social work practice. On top of what most feminists regard as the dehumanising aspects of a capitalist system, there is a centuries-old domination by masculine values. Women tend to be valued as mothers, housewives or sexual objects in 'a language that originates outside their experience' (Graham, 1983: 146). For feminist theory, therefore, 'many of the problems that women experience may be attributed to the social context rather than to internal inadequacies... 'failure to cope' might be reinterpreted as an understandable reaction to an unhealthy situation' (Donnelly, 1986: 37).

Thus, domestic violence to women is the result of social rules supporting male domination. Strauss suggests that 'our society actually has rules and values which make the marriage licence also a hitting

licence' (1977: 32). Dobash and Dobash put it this way: 'Men who assault their wives are actually living up to cultural prescriptions that are cherished in Western society - aggressiveness, male dominance and female subordination - and they are using physical force as a means to enforce that dominance' (1979: 24).

Issues arising from gender, therefore, must be regarded as fundamental to all considerations affecting women, and the relationship between a woman's personal situation and the joint context of her gender and place in society is crucial to an understanding of any problems she may face.

The conclusion of a cultural analysis of domestic violence by Campbell is that 'there is not a simple linear correlation between female status and the rates of wife assault' (1992: 19). Similarly, a review of studies in the United States by Dutton would suggest that 'the large majority (90%) of men raised under patriarchal norms are non-assaultive and non-dominant. Clearly, some individual difference factor must operate to discriminate these men (the 9.4% assaulters) from non-assaultive men' (1995: 39). He maintains that unsocial factors do indeed shape both male and female violence... The overwhelming weight of evidence supports the view that violence in intimate relationships is a learned phenomenon" (ibid: 295). For Dunon it is a combination of broad cultural values, the informal and formal social and economic structures that surround individuals and interactions within the family unit that create domestic violence. Smith suggests that 20% of wife assault might be attributed to the effects of patriarchy (1990), whilst Dunon and Starzomski assert that 20% could be attributed to psychological factors (1993).

These studies give a balancing perspective to the feminist analysis. However, it should be added that the social worker's role in the feminist analysis is to assist women to understand their problems in the

light of their position and use the insights of feminist theory as the means of resolving their difficulties.

More will be said of the implications of this thinking in what follows, but it emphasises the importance for social workers to be agents of change for clients and in society, raising the consciousness and understanding of clients, assisting them in reasserting control over their own lives and influencing society to change in ways which may seem necessary to reduce individual and collective distress, and indeed damage to the fabric of society.

This thinking is central to a final theory which would seem to offer the best overall approach to social workers as they address domestic violence - Freire's ideas of education for liberation and conscientisation. Freire suggests that knowledge can only truly be gained in a concrete and practical manner, through what he termed the praxis of action and reflection by the learner her/himself (1972 [1] and [2]). He decried theoretical or idealistic teaching (for which read 'social work') imposed by well-intentioned teachers (for which read 'social workers'). The latter are open to the accusations of cultural invasion or insensitivity and propaganda. Learners, and teachers, must become more acutely aware of a critical consciousness of reality. 'They are creators of their own learning, who respond actively through dialogue rather than mechanically and passively to the anti-dialogue of imposed, dehumanising, massified education ' (1972 (1): 29).

But Freire came to recognise that conscientisation rarely emerges through a totally personal or psychological process of renewal or change. To be real or effective conscientisation needs to emerge through reflection of a collective nature into action. Learners have to be consciously in and of the world in order to place their mark on the world. Many people inherit strong pressures against that knowledge, power and subsequent equality of dialogue which enables them to transform their

experience and fashion a destiny of their own. This dialogue is necessary if people are to take a rightful share of power in their world and in their own lives.

This theme will be expounded in further detail later, but considerable weight is added to it if one looks at the findings of Levinson's world-wide cross cultural study of family violence (1989). His conclusions suggest that adult women are at the greatest risk of family violence and that it arises from sexual jealousy, what he terms 'cause' or the will of the perpetrator. Violence is seen as part of a broader pattern of violent inter-personal conflict-resolution in the community and economic inequality is a strong predictor of wife-beating, particularly when associated with male dominance in family decision-making and restrictions on wives obtaining divorces.

The evidence of Levinson's study lends most support to theories incorporating ideas of resources, patriarchy and social learning. Resource theory sees power in marital relationships being determined by the relative value of the resources each partner brings into the relationship. Patriarchy involves concepts of feminism and male domination in society and within the family. Social learning theory argues that aggression is learned and takes place in a social context.

The existence of the four factors of a pattern of violent conflict-resolution in society, economic inequality, male dominance in decision-making and restrictions on female divorce are together a recipe for domestic violence. In terms of resolving incidents Levinson indicates that 'immediate intervention designed to stop the beating or to prevent it from ever starting is a key first line of defence' (ibid: 99). Quick intervention by relatives, neighbours or friends as mediators or providers of asylum is the best approach to reducing the amount of violence. Public censure, judicial intervention and divorce have a place but tend to intervene only after violence has persisted and often is out of all control. Immediate

protection is vital. The responses to this survey lend strong support to such advice. However, Levinson found that it is just those societies where factors predisposing women to domestic violence are prevalent that offer the least chance of such assistance. He too concludes that the main thrust of intervention should be that of a socio-economic structural approach building on the provision of a ready access to support.

Levinson's conclusions are supported by Mama who from her review of the international literature suggests:

1. that the physical abuse of women occurs across most if not all cultures and religious groups, although the local forms and dynamics have culturally specific content;

2. that it also occurs across many nations and therefore within a variety of social and political conditions;

3. that the abuse of women occurs across all socio-economic classes, even though its manifestations within different classes may vary:

4. that the degree to which violence against women by their male partners is tolerated by the dominant institutions varies considerably according to the political character of the regime in power. (1989: 19)

Sixteen societies sampled by Levinson had family lives free of violence. They were marked by several characteristics, including the following - shared domestic decision-making; some economic control by women; equal opportunity to divorce; no double standards of behaviour. and the general solution of disputes in society by peaceful means. Thus equality, sharing, co-operation and commitment and respect for each other should be the hallmarks for a society free of domestic violence - no easy prescription for the present United Kingdom cultures.

FINDINGS FROM A SMALL SURVEY OF THE EXPERIENCE OF DOMESTIC VIOLENCE BY ASIAN AND WHITE EUROPEAN WOMEN IN BIRMINGHAM

Most respondents in both groups had remained in their violent relationship for up to five years. Two Asian survivors had remained in such a relationship for between ten and fifteen years, whilst none of the White European women had remained so long.

Reasons given on both sides for remaining in a situation of domestic violence were to do with the survivors' perception of their responsibilities, i.e. children, how much control they would have over their lives if they did leave and/or how much control other people would have over them through means of power via culture or finances.

The responses of Asian women were expressed exclusively in a negative sense of their position in marriage, family and society. In common with White European women, fear of the consequences of leaving were quoted. Seven Asian respondents were clear that their reasons fell within their understanding of the term 'cultural' while others cite ignorance of help available, parental force and even, in one case, a feeling of being imprisoned as their reasons.

The significant divergence of experience between Asian and White European women, however, lies in the specific naming of their own property as a reason for staying. Two White European women responded in this way, indicating that they felt they would be leaving themselves less secure and more disempowered should they leave.

A range of responses from White European women would appear to indicate a mindset which leads them to believe that loving the man/ trying to make the marriage work/ hoping for a change in his behaviour would eventually result in the cessation of the abuse. This could indicate a clear cultural bias for White European women whereby responsibility for a good marriage is felt to rest with them. This scenario is amply illustrated in cheap novels and Hollywood movies.

Two members of each group found no-one in whom to confide, but all the rest in both groups found friends or family. However. in the instance of friends, White European women were able to talk to them three times the extent of the Asian women. This could indicate the greater opportunity for free association, less defined by culture, in Western society. One White European woman confided in the police and one in a lawyer; one Asian woman spoke to her employer. This possibly reflects perceptions of whom Asian or White European women regard as reliable figures of authority in whom they may confide, but the results do not indicate any clear conclusions. Probably the main point which needs re-emphasising, though, are the similarities rather than the differences between the responses, and the fact that the Asian women in this respect did not seem isolated.

The advice received on both sides included advice to seek help. The difference was that Asian women had been offered specific options and suggestions of help available. In the Asian women's case a significant minority of advisers (20%) had stressed the woman's responsibility to stay where she belonged and try to save the marriage. Both groups received strong advice to get out of the marriage, almost exclusively so in the case of White European women, where in one instance the advice received was to throw the husband out - perhaps inferring a greater power on the White European women's part. This point is related to the issue of economic independence: the woman in this case being the owner of the house.

In giving a yes/no answer as to whether there was pressure to conceal the abusive behaviour, more Asian women (6: 4) answered this was not so, thus apparently negating the stereotype of family pressures exerted on women in the Asian community. At the same time. and significantly, comments offered by the remaining members of the Asian group who admitted to such pressure indicated quite forceful manipulation from members of their family. "I was always escorted by members of my husband's family". "I was told not to tell anyone outside the family". "I couldn't tell other members of the family due to cultural reasons". The White European women, on the other hand, elaborated rather in terms of their own wish to conceal the abuse and their feelings of shame. "I tried to conceal what was happening as I was hoping it would cease". "I was too ashamed of what was happening to confide in anyone". "Yes, because I was ashamed".

About two thirds of each sample cited their own personal safety as the reason for leaving the situation of domestic violence, while the remainder added a concern for the safety of their children. The answers all revealed an escalation of violence after a period of time. "I couldn't live with this any longer". "I tried to kill myself after he pushed me downstairs".

The survey indicated a marked difference, however, in the manner in which each group of survivors left their situation. For Asian women, more statutory agencies were involved and to a greater extent. A total of seven Asian women used statutory agencies which varied from the local school, the Neighbourhood Office, the health clinic and the police (three instances). Most of the White European women, on the other hand, resolved their situation by either ordering their husbands out of the house or leaving home with the support of family members. In one case legal advice was sought and in two cases the police were called in.

The answers seem to suggest that the White European women, for all the pressures on them, were more able to assert themselves when their situation had deteriorated too far. None of the Asian women felt able to order their husbands out of the house and far more depended on the active involvement of statutory agencies.

Both groups responded in similar fashion to the questions about the agencies from which they sought and received help. Though more White European women subsequently sought help from the police than Asian women (5: 3), the two major discrepancies were the number of Asian women who sought help from refuges (4: 1), and actually received help (6: 2): and the larger number of White European women who sought and received help from solicitors (6: 3). These differences are not really comparable and are probably accounted for by the fact that the majority of the White European women were interviewed in a solicitor's office and the majority of the Asian women were interviewed in an Asian women's refuge. All the answers seemed to indicate that the referrals to the respective agencies were well directed insofar as all reported they received some help wherever they went.

White European women reported a universally positive reception – "I was treated sympathetically". "The police were very good". "Very well". The Asian respondents indicated a much wider variation with four very positive and two fairly positive replies - "Quite helpful". "Fair". Two responses were mixed - "Not too helpful". "Certain members of staff were very helpful but some were not" - and one experience was wholly negative - "The refuge turned me away... really awful". Such a difference may again be explained by the samples chosen and hence the settings, agencies and individuals involved.

There were no substantial differences in the child-bearing patterns of the two groups, apart from one Asian woman who had nine children. All seven of the Asian women with children were seriously concerned about the effect of the domestic violence on their children whereas all five of the White European women whose children remained with them indicated that they were not unduly concerned or affected. This is an important difference although, as has been indicated earlier, the White European women and children were now further away in time from the actual events.

Distance in time again has some bearing on differences in the present circumstances of the two groups. All of the Asian women were still in a transitional phase with significant uncertainties about their futures. Such were the uncertainties that they seemed to indicate greater turmoil. The cultural influences, for example, were most highly marked in the situations of two women who were facing a return to Asia - either in order to escape from the violence or as a result of the one year immigration rule referred to earlier. The majority of the White European women, on the other hand, indicated a fairly settled new life.

Going some way to dispelling the belief that domestic violence creates a gulf between survivors and their family and friends, nine of the ten members in each group reported the maintenance of such contacts. The replies were not detailed enough to give an indication of the level of satisfaction of these relationships. The question was not sufficiently detailed in itself to differentiate between family and friends. The responses of the Asian women, however, seemed to indicate that a crisis in all relationships was not evident and is therefore not an inevitable consequence. "Still in contact". "I'm in contact with my friends". "One sister is very supportive".

When asked about the advice they would offer to others in their position, the answers of most Asian women reinforces the opinion of Levinson (1989), quoted earlier, that women should seek help as soon as they experience violence. "Go for help immediately". "Don't wait, get help". "Get help as soon as possible". The other responses indicate the disadvantaged position in which some Asian women find themselves as a result of not being able to speak English and their unfamiliarity with statutory and voluntary aid agencies. "I would advise women to learn to speak English and make friends to find information of what is available for women". "I think the families of Asian women need to be educated". 'I feel I have been messed about".

The overwhelming majority of both groups were sure that they had made the right decision in leaving their violent relationships. Two Asian women and one White European woman were not sure whether they had made the right decision. One Asian woman, who still faced the alternative of a return to the abusive relationship or deportation felt she had chosen wrongly.

A short summary

Contrary to the hypotheses at the start of the survey, it would seem that the Asian respondents did not experience any more widespread pressures to maintain silence in the face of domestic violence than the White European respondents. Where it did occur, however, the pressure would seem to have been more coercive. Six of the Asian respondents had been born in the United Kingdom and thus may have become more influenced by Western ideas. It would appear significant that the two Asian women who expressed most fear were two who were born in Asia and faced a return there.

Such evidence as was provided by the survey would support the hypotheses that Asian women are more likely to remain in violent relationships for a longer period than White Europeans.

There may still be Asian women locked, metaphorically or even literally, in their own homes but this evidence suggests that many have their networks of family and friends who provide advice and support. It would seem that it is no longer wise automatically to think of discrete and divergent cultures but rather of various traditions with a tendency to converge, particularly for Asians born in the United Kingdom. Such a view echoes that voiced earlier in this thesis about the inter-relatedness of the specifically Asian cultures.

The answers from the Asian women, for example in the advice they would give to others in their position and in their description of their present circumstances, confirm the hypothesis that culturespecific agencies would be the best response to the issue of domestic violence, but because of the sampling it is not possible to maintain from this survey that Asian women lack this support. Overall, however, Asian respondents still present a picture of more pathos, drama and extreme suffering than their White European counterparts even when allowance is made for the differences in sampling which have been previously explained.

VI

SOME CONCLUSIONS AND SUGGESTIONS

This review would suggest the following conclusions:

1. The White European experience as documented suggests that social workers should take a sharply focused attitude on the issue of domestic violence which is essentially structurally and culturally caused. This focus, however, should not preclude an eclectic use of theory and practice, notwithstanding criticisms in the field that eclecticism can hinder a proper focus.

2. The experience of women from the ethnic minority communities, both in this and previous studies, indicates that they undergo added cultural pressures.

3. These findings emphasise for social workers the dangers of:
    - manipulating survivors into an accommodation to their situations
    - identifying failures of adjustment which require fixing for which they have the answers
    - introducing feelings of blame or guilt in relation to norms of adequate social functioning
    - reinforcing dominant and unjust cultural patterns and social structures that preclude access to information and self-realisation.

4   It seems more appropriate that a social work approach should be based on:
    - recognition of the political and cultural factors which shape all our lives

- a dynamic process of working alongside survivors and helping them to understand those forces which have shaped their lives

- recognition of the influence of the masculine domination of present cultures whilst avoiding a narrow feminist ideology which may be inimical to many survivors' thinking

- avoidance of a political correctness which precludes the recognition and confrontation of violence in relationships for fear of accusations of racism

- affirmation of survivors as the source of their own resolution of difficulties

- acceptance of the social workers' role as agents of change for individuals and society as they assist survivors in re-asserting control over their own lives and influencing society to reduce the structural and cultural factors fostering domestic violence

- incorporation of Freire's thinking which emphasises the avoidance of cultural invasion and idealistic teaching in favour of a critical consciousness of reality and the creation of people's own learning through dialogue and reflection, thus transforming their experience and fashioning their own destiny. Clients become players, not merely spectators. in a process of active reflection and reflective action.

- incorporation, therefore, of the philosophy of conscientisation which involves the re-creation of one's self-image, the validation or rejection of one's own cultural base, the withdrawal from self-defeating or negative attitudes and behaviour and the refusal to accept unfair or self-damaging conditions of life

- realisation that in pursuit of this goal culture-specific voluntary agencies with peer-group training in the field are the social workers' best allies in this mission and a sine qua non for effective action - a view supported by Parmar in her own recent thesis on this subject (1995: 17).

5.   The findings of the small survey conducted as part of this thesis indicate that it would be useful to continue to investigate the experiences of the survivors of domestic violence in all the cultures and communities in the United Kingdom. Such studies, apart from providing further evidence of needs and resources in this field, would help to monitor what appear to be continuing changes in cultural patterns and test the notion which has emerged in this review of some convergence of experience both within the Asian communities and between ethnic minority communities in general and White European cultures. There is also a tantalising hint that there might be a growing readiness among Asian women in the United Kingdom both to reject violence in domestic relationships and to do so sooner than in the past. A more comprehensive study is necessary, however, to substantiate such a view.

BIBLIOGRAPHY

Amin, K. 1928, *Tahrir al Marta (The Liberation of Women)*, Umum-al-Makatib Bimisr Walharij

Bart, P.B. & Moran. E.G.(Eds.), 1993 *Violence Against Women: The Bloody Footprints*, Sage

Belgrave Baheno, 1995, *The Manushi Report: Beaten But Not Defeated* Belgrave Baheno

BBC Radio 4, 1995, *Islam - A Faith to Question*, File on Four

Bryan. B., Dadzie S. & Scafe, S. 1985, *The Heart of the Race: Black Women's Lives in Britain*, Virago

Bush T. & Hood-Williams,J., 1995, *Domestic Violence on a London Housing Estate*, Research Bulletin No. 37. Home Office Research and Statistics Department pp 11-18, HMSO

Campbell J. 1992, 'Prevention of Wife Battering: Insights from Cultural Analysis' *Response*, 14(3) pp18-24

Deltufo A. 1995, *Domestic Violence for Beginners*, Writers & Readers Publishing Inc.

Dobash R.E. & Dobash R.P., 1979, *Violence Against Wives: A Case Against the Patriarchy* Free Press

Donnelly A., 1986, *Feminist Social Work with a Women's Group*, Social Work Monograph No. 41, University of East Anglia

Dutton D.G., 1995, *The Domestic Assault: Psychological and Criminal Justice Perspectives*, University of British Columbia Press

Dutton D.G. & Starzomski, A., 1993 'Borderline Personality Organisation in Perpetrators of Psychological and Physical Abuse'. *Violence and Victims*, 8 (4), pp 327-338

Freire P., 1972(1), *Cultural Action for Freedom*, Penguin

Freire P., 1972(2), *Pedagogy of the Oppressed*, Herder & Herder

Graham H. 1983 "Do Her Answers Fit His Questions? Women and the Survey Method" in Garmarnikow E. et al, *The Public and the Private*, Heinemann

Herbert M., 1981, *Behavioural Treatment of Problem Children: A Practice Manual*, Academic Press

Hollis F., 1964, *Casework: A Psychosocial Therapy*, Random House Press

Howe, D., 1987, *An Introduction to Social Work Theory: Making Sense in Pratice*, Ashgate

Howe D., 1991 'Knowledge, Power and the Shape of Social Work Practice', in Davies M., (Ed.), *The Sociology of Social Work,* Routledge and Kegan Paul

Hudson B. L. & Macdonald. G. M. 1986, *Behavioural Social Work: An Introduction* Macmillan

James. S. M. & Busia P. A. (Eds.), 1993, *Theorising Black Feminisms,* Routledge

Levinson D., 1989, *Family Violence in Cross-Cultural Perspective,* Sage

Liebow E., 1967, *Tally's Corner,* Little Brown

Mama A., 1989, *The Hidden Struggle: Statutory and Voluntary Sector Responses to Violence Against Black Women in the Home*, Race and Housing Research Unit

Masson J., 1993 *Against Therapy,* Harper-Collins

McCann M. C., 1995, *Woman Battering and Feminist Critiques: Implications for Social Work Practice*, Unpublished Thesis - University College, Dublin

Mernissi F., 1975, *Beyond the Veil: Male-Female Dynamics in a Modern Muslim Society Schenkman*

Morley R. & Mullender A., 1994, *Preventing Domestic Violence to Women*, Home Office Police Research Group

Mirrlees-Black C., 1995, "Estimating the Extent of Domestic Violence: Findings from the 1992 British Crime Survey". *Research Bulletin No. 37*. Home Office Research and Statistics Department, pp 1-9 HMSO

Pahl J., (Ed.) 1985, *Private Violence and Public Policy,* Routledge & Kegan Paul

Parmar B., 1995, *Domestic Violence From A Female Asian Perspective*, Unpublished Thesis, University of Leicester

Parmar P., 1982, 'Gender, Race and Class: Asian Women in Resistance', in *The Empire Strikes Back: Racism 1970-79*. Centre for Contemporary Studies (Eds) Hutchison

Perlman H., 1957, *Casework: A Problem-Solving Approach*, University of Chicago Press

Reid W. & Epstein L., 1972, *Task-Centred Casework,* Columbia University Press

Rowe D., 1993, Foreword in Masson, J., *Against Therapy* Harper-Collins

Sahgal G., 1990, 'Fundamentalism and the Multi-Culturalist Fallacy', in *Against the Grain,* Southall Black Sisters

Smith L., 1989, 'Domestic Violence', *Home Office Research Study no. 107* HMSO

Smith M., 1990, 'Patriarchal Ideology and Wife-Beating: A Test of Feminist Hypotheses', *Violence and Victims*, 5 (4) pp 257-273

Southall Black Sisters Collective (Eds.), 1990, *Against the Grain: A Celebration of Survival and Struggle. Southall Black Sisters 1979-1989,*   Southall Black Sisters

Southall Black Sisters Collective (Eds.) no date, *Domestic Violence and Asian Women - An Information Pack,* Southall Black Sisters

Stack C., 1974, *All Our Kin: Strategies for Survival in a Black Community*, Harper & Row

Strauss M. A., 1977, 'Violence in the Family: How Widespread, Why it Occurs and Some Thoughts on Prevention', in *Family Violence: Proceedings from a Symposium*, United Way of Greater Vancouver

Stelrnan A., 1993, 'Domestic violence: Old Crime, Sudden Interest', *in Probation Journal*, vol. 40 no. 4, pp 193-198, National Association of Probation Officers

Taylor P.V., 1993, *The Texts of Paula Freire*, Open University Press

WAITS, 1995, *Freedom From Abuse: Domestic Violence in the Asian, African-Caribbean and Arab Communities*, WAITS

Wallis J., 1973, *Personal Counselling: An Introduction to Relationship Theory*, Allen & Unwin

Wilson A., 1978, *Finding a Voice: Asian Women in Britain*, Virago Press

SOCIAL WORK MONOGRAPHS

are published by

**The School of Social Work at
the University of East Anglia,
Norwich, NR4 7TJ**

For information about titles (including our
highly-regarded Law Files),
or to obtain an uptodate checklist,
write to
The Social Work Monograph office at this
address,
or phone 01603 592068 or 592087